1st Grade Math Workbooks:
Addition & Subtraction

SPEEDY
PUBLISHING

Speedy Publishing LLC
40 E. Main St. #1156
Newark, DE 19711
www.speedypublishing.com

Simple Addition of single-digit numbers

1. 3 + 8 = _____

2. 7 + 5 = _____

3. 7 + 6 = _____

4. 6 + 4 = _____

5. 7 + 3 = _____

6. 9 + 9 = _____

7. 2 + 5 = _____

8. 6 + 8 = _____

9. $8 + 9 =$ ____

10. $9 + 8 =$ ____

11. $5 + 9 =$ ____

12. $5 + 5 =$ ____

13. $1 + 1 =$ ____

14. $7 + 4 =$ ____

15. $5 + 2 =$ ____

16. $3 + 9 =$ ____

17. $7 + 8 =$ ____

18. $5 + 1 =$ ____

19. $5 + 4 =$ ____

20. $5 + 2 =$ ____

21. 3 + 6 = ____

22. 2 + 3 = ____

23. 0 + 2 = ____

24. 6 + 5 = ____

25. 6 + 9 = ____

26. 4 + 3 = ____

27. 6 + 3 = ____

28. 7 + 5 = ____

29. 5 + 0 = ____

30. 0 + 6 = ____

31. 4 + 0 = ____

32. 4 + 5 = ____

33. 8 + 2 = ____

39. 1 + 6 = ____

34. 8 + 5 = ____

40. 9 + 2 = ____

35. 2 + 4 = ____

41. 5 + 8 = ____

36. 4 + 1 = ____

42. 3 + 3 = ____

37. 7 + 5 = ____

43. 0 + 5 = ____

38. 3 + 1 = ____

44. 9 + 4 = ____

45. $9 + 8 =$ _____

51. $3 + 9 =$ _____

46. $2 + 7 =$ _____

52. $2 + 5 =$ _____

47. $4 + 9 =$ _____

53. $5 + 5 =$ _____

48. $3 + 4 =$ _____

54. $6 + 6 =$ _____

49. $7 + 8 =$ _____

55. $7 + 3 =$ _____

50. $7 + 9 =$ _____

56. $4 + 7 =$ _____

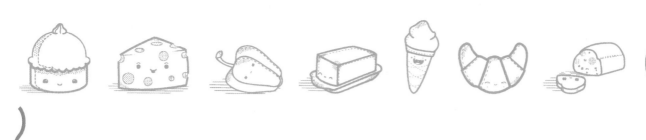

57. 4 + 0 = ____

58. 3 + 6 = ____

59. 1 + 5 = ____

60. 5 + 4 = ____

61. 0 + 8 = ____

62. 6 + 9 = ____

63. 6 + 3 = ____

64. 5 + 8 = ____

65. 1 + 7 = ____

66. 4 + 3 = ____

67. 2 + 1 = ____

68. 1 + 5 = ____

69. 9 + 6 = _____

75. 0 + 2 = _____

70. 4 + 0 = _____

76. 5 + 8 = _____

71. 1 + 6 = _____

77. 5 + 5 = _____

72. 2 + 0 = _____

78. 0 + 7 = _____

73. 5 + 2 = _____

79. 1 + 4 = _____

74. 6 + 5 = _____

80. 3 + 4 = _____

Adding 3 numbers

1. 4 + 2 + 1 = ____

2. 8 + 3 + 4 = ____

3. 4 + 2 + 6 = ____

4. 1 + 1 + 1 = ____

5. 2 + 3 + 7 = ____

6. 8 + 2 + 4 = ____

7. 5 + 4 + 6 = ____

8. 1 + 1 + 5 = ____

9. 2 + 4 + 2 = ____

10. 1 + 3 + 5 = ____

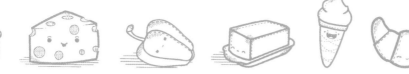

11. $2 + 5 + 1 =$ _____

17. $6 + 1 + 3 =$ _____

12. $1 + 6 + 1 =$ _____

18. $1 + 1 + 3 =$ _____

13. $5 + 3 + 2 =$ _____

19. $2 + 4 + 6 =$ _____

14. $5 + 9 + 2 =$ _____

20. $6 + 6 + 3 =$ _____

15. $2 + 3 + 0 =$ _____

21. $3 + 4 + 1 =$ _____

16. $3 + 3 + 2 =$ _____

22. $5 + 4 + 1 =$ _____

23. $5 + 0 + 1 =$ ___

29. $4 + 1 + 6 =$ ___

24. $3 + 3 + 4 =$ ___

30. $5 + 0 + 5 =$ ___

25. $5 + 3 + 4 =$ ___

31. $6 + 2 + 3 =$ ___

26. $1 + 4 + 2 =$ ___

32. $3 + 1 + 6 =$ ___

27. $4 + 0 + 8 =$ ___

33. $1 + 1 + 5 =$ ___

28. $5 + 1 + 3 =$ ___

34. $4 + 3 + 1 =$ ___

35. 6 + 1 + 2 = ____

41. 6 + 5 + 8 = ____

36. 3 + 2 + 9 = ____

42. 6 + 0 + 9 = ____

37. 3 + 3 + 9 = ____

43. 5 + 9 + 0 = ____

38. 2 + 6 + 3 = ____

44. 4 + 5 + 5 = ____

39. 4 + 1 + 7 = ____

45. 3 + 3 + 6 = ____

40. 5 + 5 + 3 = ____

46. 4 + 1 + 9 = ____

47. 1 + 6 + 5 = _____

53. 5 + 4 + 7 = _____

48. 6 + 5 + 5 = _____

54. 1 + 2 + 8 = _____

49. 4 + 2 + 6 = _____

55. 2 + 3 + 1 = _____

50. 0 + 5 + 7 = _____

56. 2 + 5 + 7 = _____

51. 4 + 2 + 5 = _____

57. 3 + 2 + 1 = _____

52. 2 + 3 + 3 = _____

58. 3 + 6 + 4 = _____

59. 1 + 5 + 5 = _____

60. 3 + 7 + 5 = _____

61. 2 + 5 + 6 = _____

62. 2 + 2 + 2 = _____

63. 6 + 2 + 5 = _____

64. 6 + 1 + 6 = _____

65. 2 + 1 + 5 = _____

66. 2 + 2 + 7 = _____

67. 0 + 1 + 8 = _____

68. 6 + 0 + 3 = _____

69. 6 + 3 + 0 = _____

70. 5 + 5 + 6 = _____

71. 4 + 8 + 4 = _____

72. 2 + 5 + 9 = _____

73. 0 + 6 + 4 = _____

74. 1 + 5 + 4 = _____

75. 6 + 2 + 9 = _____

76. 4 + 5 + 2 = _____

77. 2 + 1 + 1 = _____

78. 5 + 3 + 8 = _____

79. 6 + 7 + 4 = _____

80. 4 + 4 + 2 = _____

81. 2 + 2 + 7 = _____

82. 3 + 7 + 3 = _____

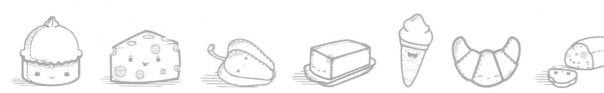

Simple Subtraction

1. 13 – 0 = _____

2. 18 – 8 = _____

3. 13 – 1 = _____

4. 16 – 14 = _____

5. 18 – 2 = _____

6. 17 – 7 = _____

7. 14 – 0 = _____

8. 14 – 4 = _____

9. 15 – 2 = _____

10. 15 – 5 = _____

11. 16 – 1 = _____

17. 19 – 2 = _____

12. 19 – 9 = _____

18. 15 – 4 = _____

13. 14 – 2 = _____

19. 19 – 5 = _____

14. 12 – 10 = _____

20. 19 – 6 = _____

15. 18 – 7 = _____

21. 18 – 6 = _____

16. 14 – 12 = _____

22. 19 – 8 = _____

23. 14 − 10 = _____   **29.** 14 − 11 = _____

24. 19 − 4 = _____   **30.** 18 − 5 = _____

25. 13 − 0 = _____   **31.** 15 − 11 = _____

26. 17 − 15 = _____   **32.** 12 − 0 = _____

27. 13 − 1 = _____   **33.** 14 − 1 = _____

28. 11 − 0 = _____   **34.** 19 − 3 = _____

35. 15 − 5 = _____

41. 16 − 2 = _____

36. 13 − 3 = _____

42. 19 − 5 = _____

37. 13 − 2 = _____

43. 19 − 4 = _____

38. 17 − 1 = _____

44. 15 − 4 = _____

39. 15 − 4 = _____

45. 13 − 1 = _____

40. 19 − 2 = _____

46. 19 − 1 = _____

47. 16 – 6 = _____

53. 15 – 0 = _____

48. 18 – 7 = _____

54. 16 – 1 = _____

49. 15 – 12 = _____

55. 19 – 0 = _____

50. 15 – 1 = _____

56. 13 – 2 = _____

51. 17 – 3 = _____

57. 14 – 0 = _____

52. 19 – 3 = _____

58. 18 – 4 = _____

59. 19 – 9 = _____

65. 19 – 7 = _____

60. 14 – 1 = _____

66. 14 – 1 = _____

61. 17 – 4 = _____

67. 13 – 3 = _____

62. 16 – 2 = _____

68. 19 – 5 = _____

63. 16 – 1 = _____

69. 19 – 6 = _____

64. 11 – 1 = _____

70. 19 – 9 = _____

71. 16 − 6 = _____

72. 16 − 4 = _____

73. 13 − 10 = _____

74. 18 − 5 = _____

75. 17 − 15 = _____

76. 14 − 4 = _____

77. 17 − 1 = _____

78. 12 − 2 = _____

79. 13 − 11 = _____

80. 16 − 0 = _____

81. 17 − 6 = _____

82. 18 − 4 = _____

Add and Subtract 3 single-digit numbers

1. 9 + 1 − 1

2. 10 + 10 − 8

3. 7 − 5 + 5

4. 4 + 9 − 2

5. 8 + 4 + 4

6. 5 + 4 + 9

7. 8 + 5 + 6

8. 4 + 2 − 1

9. 4 − 4 + 3

10. 6 + 2 − 4

11. 6 + 9 + 1

12. 9 − 8 + 4

13. 10 + 8 + 6

14. 10 + 5 + 10

15. 1 + 1 + 5

16. 9 − 2 + 7

17. 8 − 3 + 7

18. 5 + 3 + 4

19. 5 − 1 + 7

20. 2 + 10 + 9

1.	11	17.	15	33.	10
2.	12	18.	6	34.	13
3.	13	19.	9	35.	6
4.	10	20.	7	36.	5
5.	10	21.	9	37.	12
6.	18	22.	5	38.	4
7.	7	23.	2	39.	7
8.	14	24.	11	40.	11
9.	17	25.	15	41.	13
10.	17	26.	7	42.	6
11.	14	27.	9	43.	5
12.	10	28.	12	44.	13
13.	2	29.	5	45.	17
14.	11	30.	6	46.	9
15.	7	31.	4	47.	13
16.	12	32.	9	48.	7

49.	15	60.	9	71.	7
50.	16	61.	8	72.	2
51.	12	62.	15	73.	7
52.	7	63.	9	74.	11
53.	10	64.	13	75.	2
54.	12	65.	8	76.	13
55.	10	66.	7	77.	10
56.	11	67.	3	78.	7
57.	4	68.	6	79.	5
58.	9	69.	15	80.	7
59.	6	70.	4		

ANSWERS

1.	7	5.	12	9.	8
2.	15	6.	14	10.	9
3.	12	7.	15	11.	8
4.	3	8.	7	12.	8

13.	10	29.	11	45.	12
14.	16	30.	10	46.	14
15.	5	31.	11	47.	12
16.	8	32.	10	48.	16
17.	10	33.	7	49.	12
18.	5	34.	8	50.	12
19.	12	35.	9	51.	11
20.	15	36.	14	52.	8
21.	8	37.	15	53.	16
22.	10	38.	11	54.	11
23.	6	39.	12	55.	6
24.	10	40.	13	56.	14
25.	12	41.	19	57.	6
26.	7	42.	15	58.	13
27.	12	43.	14	59.	11
28.	9	44.	14	60.	15

61.	13	69.	9	77.	4
62.	6	70.	16	78.	16
63.	13	71.	16	79.	17
64.	13	72.	16	80.	10
65.	8	73.	10	81.	11
66.	11	74.	10	82.	13
67.	9	75.	17		
68.	9	76.	11		

ANSWERS

1.	13	8.	10	15.	11
2.	10	9.	13	16.	2
3.	12	10.	10	17.	17
4.	2	11.	15	18.	11
5.	16	12.	10	19.	14
6.	10	13.	12	20.	13
7.	14	14.	2	21.	12

22.	11	38.	16	54.	15
23.	4	39.	11	55.	19
24.	15	40.	17	56.	11
25.	13	41.	14	57.	14
26.	2	42.	14	58.	14
27.	12	43.	15	59.	10
28.	11	44.	11	60.	13
29.	3	45.	12	61.	13
30.	13	46.	18	62.	14
31.	4	47.	10	63.	15
32.	12	48.	11	64.	10
33.	13	49.	3	65.	12
34.	16	50.	14	66.	13
35.	10	51.	14	67.	10
36.	10	52.	16	68.	14
37.	11	53.	15	69.	13

70.	10	75.	2	80.	16
71.	10	76.	10	81.	11
72.	12	77.	16	82.	14
73.	3	78.	10		
74.	13	79.	2		

ANSWERS

1.	9	11.	16
2.	12	12.	5
3.	7	13.	24
4.	11	14.	25
5.	16	15.	7
6.	18	16.	14
7.	19	17.	12
8.	5	18.	12
9.	3	19.	11
10.	4	20.	21